I'm a Gamekeeper

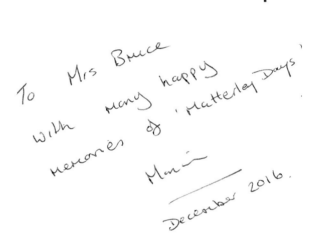

To Mrs Bruce
With many happy
Memories of 'Matterley Days'
Marion
December 2016.

Marion Kellow

Published by

MELROSE BOOKS

An Imprint of Melrose Press Limited
St Thomas Place, Ely
Cambridgeshire
CB7 4GG, UK
www.melrosebooks.co.uk

FIRST EDITION

Copyright © Marion Kellow 2016

The Author asserts her moral right to
be identified as the author of this work

Cover designed by Melrose Books

ISBN 978-1-911280-72-9
epub 978-1-911280-73-6
mobi 978-1-911280-74-3

Printed and bound in Great Britain by:
4edge Limited
7a Eldon Way, Eldon Way Industrial Estate
Hockley, Essex
SS5 4AD

Dedicated to Fred Kellow
who died on 7th November 2016
and to Rosemary Kellow, his devoted wife of 71 years.

Preface

Fred Kellow was born into a farming family in the small village of Burcombe, South Wiltshire, in 1924. His early life was dominated by the poverty that was common amongst country folk in the 1920s and 30s. It was at this time that Fred developed his love and passion for the countryside. Fred's life has been governed by the timeless rhythm of the changing seasons, in particular the shooting year, which starts in the early spring when adult pheasants are caught and lay eggs. Through the summer, chicks are reared until ready for the start of the shooting season on the 1st October. The pheasant-shooting season finishes on 1st February. There were only a few shoots in January, but during this period, Fred's attention turned towards the next rearing and shooting cycle.

Fred's family had, for several generations, lived as farm labourers and carters. They had worked on farms in and around the Nadder Valley in South Wiltshire for several hundreds of years. They were used to hard work for little reward, and life was always on the edge. When Fred was born, life was little different. The country was still suffering the effects of the Great War, which had ended just six years before, and the General Strike of 1926 was looming. However, Fred was to see and witness a pace of change like none experienced by his ancestors. General living conditions were to improve to such an extent over his lifetime that Fred would see villages change from the homes of people who lived and worked on the land to being the playgrounds of city dwellers migrating to the countryside.

Fred started his working life as a farm worker and part-time rabbit catcher. In the mid-1950s, Fred changed direction and became a gamekeeper; first at Hurdcott Estate near Barford St Martin, Wiltshire and then at Matterley Estate near Winchester in Hampshire. Throughout this time, Fred built a reputation amongst the shooting fraternity as one of the best gamekeepers of his generation. His ideas and knowledge were in much demand by other gamekeepers and shooting folk.

Fred sadly died aged 92 shortly before his story could be published. He is survived by his wife Rosemary, his son Derek and daughter Marion. He also has two granddaughters and great grandchildren. Right until his death, Fred had a keen interest in the world around him and in particular a passion for country life. He had strong views on the political and social changes that have taken place throughout his lifetime. In particular, he held strong and sometimes controversial views on the impact of these changes on the countryside. His passion was so great that he wanted his story told and his viewpoint heard in the hope that somebody might listen before the countryside he loved disappeared for ever.

Chapter 1

The man in the woodshed came every autumn for a few weeks and started Fred Kellow on a career that was to last a lifetime. The woodshed was attached to the thatched cottage where Fred was born in January 1924. His dad, also called Fred, had come to the cottage as a young boy and in 1916 brought his bride, Nancy (Annie) Moody, to live there. They raised a family of five boys and one girl and in later years the cottage saw the birth of some of their grandchildren, including Fred's first child, Derek.

In the 1920s and 30s, life was hard for the village folk of Burcombe. Fred's dad worked on the local farm as a carter and dairyman. His mum had a full-time job bringing up her six children. To make a bit of money, Fred senior had four allotments where he grew vegetables for the family. Any surplus he took into Wilton to the grocer and sold for a few shillings. He also kept chickens, which meant the family had plenty of eggs, but the majority of eggs were sold. When money was particularly short, the children would either go without or share an egg between two for breakfast. All the children had jobs to do. Every day after school, Fred helped to weed the allotments and collect the eggs. One day he tripped on the way home, dropping his bucket and breaking most of the eggs. This was devastating for his mum as there would be no pennies from the eggs that week. Fred recalled that she cried and cried.

In the autumn, their meagre funds were boosted a little by the woodshed man, who paid a few shillings for the privilege of living in their woodshed. He came during September, October and November, which was rabbiting time! Fred loved rabbiting and went with him whenever he could. The Burcombe downs around the punchbowl were covered in trees and scrub in those days. That changed in 1940, when Italian prisoners of war were set to use clearing the land. All the scrub and bushes were cleared and the land ploughed up to grow crops, turning the downs into the rolling farmland we see today.

There were hundreds and hundreds of rabbits in the 1930s, so the woodshed man and Fred had an important job, culling the rabbits before the countryside was overrun with them. The woodshed man taught Fred how to set the wires and where to put them. They put the wires on tracks where the rabbits wandered. The wires were set and checked every day. They would set their wires over a section of the downs and after a couple of days move around to another section. This continued until the whole down had been wired, at which point they would start at the beginning again.

Rabbits formed part of the staple diet for most people; rabbit stew, fried rabbit, and rabbit sandwiches. There was always somebody willing to pay a few shillings for a couple of rabbits. Sometimes Fred would go out catching rabbits on his own, something he was not supposed to do. Occasionally, Wilton Park gamekeepers caught him, resulting in a telling off and threats to get his parents evicted, but nothing ever happened. His mum took a few rabbits for the family each week and sold the rest to add a few pence to the family's earnings. Fred never got a penny for his efforts. Rabbits, vegetables, eggs and milk, which came from the farm, were usually available. There were no shops in Burcombe so villagers had to either go to Barford St Martin, Wilton or Salisbury, or rely on the traders who frequently came to the village. The grocer and baker came round the village every day. Fred's mum would give him a list of what she wanted and he would deliver the goods the next day. On Saturday evenings, about six o'clock, Fred's dad would go to the market in Salisbury. Usual purchases were a shoulder of bacon for about three shillings, and salt fish. The fish he took to the withy beds and put in the river for 24 hours to wash the salt out before cooking.

The river was also used for washing, but only in the summer. Fred would take a bar of soap and stand in the river and wash. This was nothing unusual; all the Burcombe folk used the river for bathing. In the winter it was far too cold. Heating water was a hard and labour-intensive job. Wood for the fire had to be gathered from the downs and water drawn from the well. Fred's mum would go out wood-gathering every couple of weeks. She and her friend would take prams and, with the children, go out to collect wood for the fire. This was used to stoke up the copper and to boil the washing.

Food was short for the family, as it was for most people in the village, and they had to live on a limited diet, in terms of both quantity and variety. Breakfast was usually half an egg with toast and pork dripping. Occasionally the children had bacon as the family kept their own pigs. On school days Fred took a sandwich, maybe a bit of cheese or rabbit. After school there was usually homemade cake to eat and sometimes, but certainly not always, a hot meal of some sort. Frequently he went without a cooked meal or tea! This was usually because he got into some trouble, maybe over the eggs or something else. On those days, Fred would clear off out of the house and hang about somewhere else in the village until it was getting dark. When he got home, he would then get a clout and be sent to bed without food. Luckily, the pantry was at the bottom of the stairs and he would sneak down and pinch something to eat. That's if he could get away without one of his four brothers snitching on him! Then he would be in trouble all over again.

At Christmas, the family would have one of their chickens for Christmas dinner and Fred's mum always made Christmas puddings. Throughout the year, the family contributed to the Thrift Club. This was run for the village by Fred's dad and it meant people had a little extra to buy a few special bits and pieces. There were oranges, nuts and chocolate for the children's stockings and maybe a small present.

Some of the wealthier people of the village tried to help a little. For example, the vicar had two servant girls, and every day they sat on the vicarage steps with jugs of beef tea and gave to any who needed it. There were loads of children living in the village and on Saturday mornings they would all troop down the road to Mrs Vine's house, where they were each given one sweet; a very special treat.

There were always lots of people and traders coming through the village. One of the favourites was the hurdy-gurdy man. He would stand outside the Ship Inn, opposite Fred's house, and play his barrel organ. His monkey would sit quietly until it heard its tune then it would hop and skip about, dancing. This always brought squeals of delight from the children. Another special event was Bonfire Night. Mr Spearings at the Old Mill always did the fireworks for the village. There would be a bonfire of sorts, burning up old rubbish and a few rockets. It was modest by today's standards, but a huge event in those days.

The Old Mill had a small stream running alongside it and was full of fresh water oysters, thousands of them. Twice, Fred found pearls in the shells but, not understanding their value, threw them back into the river! If any money had been gained from them it would have been added to the family's funds. On one occasion on the allotments, Fred found a gold sovereign. This was taken off him and was used to pay for a taxi for the whole family to visit his grandparents at Lockerley.

On school days, Fred would walk with all the children along Burcombe Lane to go to school in Barford St Martin. At the end of the lane, they climbed over the stile and went across the water meadows. In the summer, on nice, fine, warm days, it was a pleasant walk, but it was a different story in the winter months when it was wet and cold. It was only in the very worst of weather that the children could stay home. On wet days when they arrived at school the children had to stand in front of the radiators to get dry! Teachers were very liberal with their use of the cane in those days and lateness was greeted with a caning. Persistent lateness, or even one day's absence, would result in a visit from the School Attendance Officer (SAO). Every day the SAO would cycle from Tisbury to Wilton, calling into every school on the way to check the registers and then visiting the home of any absentee. Children and adults alike were fearful of his visit.

Fred's time at school was fairly turbulent, as he got into many scrapes and was on the wrong end of many canings. There was one incident at Wilton School where Fred fell out with his woodwork teacher. Fred had a chisel in his hand and threw it at the teacher. Realising what he had done, Fred leapt out the window and sped off, chased by some of his classmates who were sent after him. He was caught and marched back to school to be caned.

Fred's reflections on his time at Wilton are quite vivid:

I had the cane when I was at Wilton School and that was severe punishment. They used to hit you bloody hard. Everybody said how hard they hit you. The headmaster would hold your hand and hit you. Once I pulled my hand away and he hit his own bloody hand. Christ, didn't he go for me then. But he hopped! I didn't half cop it. They'd give you the cane for virtually anything; talking in class. What the teacher did was send you to stand outside the door. The headmaster would walk around and pick you up and sort you out. Buggers they were, they treated you bad.

Around this time, electricity came to Burcombe. Oil lamps were replaced with electric light, but the main advantage for Fred was the wireless! Up to this time the family had a wireless that had an accumulator. The boys would take the accumulator up the road to George Burton who would charge it up. However, the big problem was there were only two sets of headphones! The boys and their father were big fans of boxing and on fight nights they all wanted to listen to the fight broadcast. This inevitably led to fights in the living room as they squabbled over the headphones. So a wireless that they could all sit and listen to was a huge bonus for the family.

Fred left school at the age of 14 and joined the building trade. As the 'boy', he was often asked to do dangerous things; for example, when they set the hoist up on building sites he had to ride up on it to see if it worked! After about eight months his time with the builder came to an abrupt end. The boss' son oversaw him. One morning, Fred turned up for work on time, but he had to wait for the boss' son to turn up. To pass the time he idly took some small tacks and with a hammer started tapping the tacks into the workbench. The next thing he knew he was getting boxed around his ears. In an instant he turned and lashed out, clouting his assailant on the head with his hammer. The boss' son was knocked out cold. Knowing his time was up, Fred handed in his notice.

He then went to work for Jack Coombes at Barford St Martin, where he was to stay for the next 20 years. It was immediately obvious to Jack that Fred was interested in rabbiting, so for most of the winter months that was what he did, along with trapping and killing vermin. Throughout the summer he worked on the farm. During the week, all the rabbits went to the farm and were sold, but at weekends Fred was allowed to catch rabbits for himself. This he did, and after supplying the family he would sell what was left.

At the outbreak of World War II, Fred tried to enlist, but was refused as he was in a reserved occupation. So instead, along with his older brother David, he joined the Burcombe Home Guard. They went training every Sunday morning and one night a week, and didn't miss it without having some serious explaining to do! Their job was to look out for any German parachutists. To this end they used a hut on top of the downs as their observation post. The nearest telephone was in the village, so Fred acted as a runner, sprinting to the village to Sidney Pond's house to raise the alarm. Fred was a very good runner and throughout the War and beyond he entered all the races in the district, winning them all and pocketing the prize money.

Burcombe Homeguard was made up of young men who were either in reserved occupations or too young to enlist, or older men who were too old for the regular army. However, most of the older men had seen service in World War I. In command was the local farmer, Sidney Pond, who had a telephone and a car! However, he did not always have the respect of his troops. Fred remembers, '*If we went on church parade, he was the only bugger out of step*'. The RSM was Fred Chalk, who had been an RSM in the marines in World War I. He was a totally different character and when he spoke everyone took notice.

Later in the War, Fred was promoted to the rank of Corporal. Under his command was an ex-World War I captain, an ex-Lieutenant and an ex-prisoner of war. One of their drills was to man a roadblock, if looking for escaped prisoners or parachutists. As Corporal, Fred had to stand in the open to challenge suspects, whilst the others hid and provided cover. Fred was supposed to shout, '*Halt!*' If there was no reply he had to shout it again and if there was still no reply his men would open fire. This was all rather nerve-wracking for a very young corporal, but the old-timers instilled some confidence by saying, '*Don't worry nipper, we'll shoot them.*'

Occasionally, throughout the War, the Homeguard had to attend military training with the regular army. Straightaway, they were given a live hand grenade each. Then they had to lie on the ground and throw their grenade, never looking up to see if it went off. The RSM shouted at them, '*Don't forget to keep your arses down or you'll get hit in the arse with shrapnel!*' At first, Fred had a 12 bore shotgun and he was then issued with a Thompson machine gun. Later, this was taken back by the army and he was given a rifle. The Homeguard had to get in line and advance on a target while live bullets were fired at the ground, kicking up the dirt just in front of them. Fred recalled that there were always a couple of ambulances nearby!

When Fred was promoted to Corporal he was put in charge of a Black Bombard mortar, which fired a 28-pound infantry shell or an anti-tank shell. It had a 400-yard range and an 18-ton recoil. In order to hold it still, it had long iron pegs that had to be driven into the ground. On one training exercise a regular army officer asked Fred what he would do if he ran out of ammunition and the Germans were advancing. Fred's retort was, '*I'd run like hell!*' This caused a great deal of laughter.

At the beginning of the War, regular army soldiers were put with the Homeguard. However, this proved problematic and after a short while this practice stopped.

Ruffle and Wallis were on duty with two regular army soldiers, manning the observation hut on the downs. Wallis was a farmer and Ruffle a schoolteacher and they didn't want to sleep in the hut so they went for a walk around the downs. The two soldiers stayed in the hut and when they saw those two coming back, they shot at them! There was a barn not far from there, so Wallis and Ruffle ran to the barn and waited. The soldiers called up their HQ and we were all called out. They said they knew where the Germans were, in the barn. We surrounded the barn, starting about half a mile from it and crept up on them. The RSM shouted, 'Come out or we'll throw a grenade in!' 'Don't do that, it's only us,' shouted Wallis and Ruffle. Bloody soldiers shot at our own men.

One bus journey home from Salisbury, during the middle of the War years, was to have the most profound impact of all on young Fred. It was on this bus journey that he was drawn to a young brunette, Rosemary Mullins, who was chatting to her friend. As he stepped off the bus, Fred cheekily said to her, *'See you next Thursday, six o'clock at the bus station.'* The following week she turned up, but had to explain that her last bus home to Ansty was in half an hour. The following weekend there was a dance in Swallowcliff, so Fred and Rose agreed to meet by the maypole in Ansty.

So Fred made his first journey to Ansty, cycling all the way, a distance of about nine miles, most of which was an uphill climb. He waited by the maypole, much to the curiosity of the Ansty village folk, who wondered what this handsome young stranger was up to. From then on, he became a familiar figure in the village, attending all the local dances with Rosemary. His cycle home was at times precarious, having to ride in darkness as only very dim lights were allowed during the war years. During these night rides, he watched the searchlights, looking for German bombers. At the end of the war, Fred and Rose got married in St John's Church in Ansty. Their honeymoon was on the coast at Christchurch, staying with Fred's Auntie Kate. She came to the wedding and wanted some rabbits so, on his wedding day, Fred was up early and out rabbiting! On return from their honeymoon, Fred and Rose lived with his mum and dad in the cottage at Burcombe. It was here in March the following year that Fred and Rose's son, Derek, was born.

During the war years, farms were not allowed to rear pheasants so Fred concentrated on killing the rabbits and controlling vermin; there were plenty of them around. Fred had a gross of wires (144 in total) and he would set them in the same place for two days' running and then move the wires to a new area. Each night he caught about 40 rabbits. After an area had been wired he would take his ferrets out to the warrens. Nets were placed over all the holes and then the ferrets were put down the holes to hunt the rabbits. The rabbits would charge out of the holes and into the nets. In rabbit warrens where it was hard to hunt with ferrets, Fred used gin traps instead.[1]

---

1 A gin trap was a metal trap used to catch small mammals. These traps have now been banned, but were commonly used at this time.

Rabbits were a vital part of the diet during the war years. Food rationing was harsh, so anything that was not rationed was very welcome. Fred's mum had four rabbits each week and Fred would get them for anybody else who wanted them. However, most village folk poached a few rabbits for themselves. Most of Fred's rabbits were sold to a dealer from Reading. He would come on Sundays and collect any rabbits and also chickens if Fred had any. This continued after the war. Fred also had some regular customers for his rabbits around the village of Barford. When he and Rose moved to their first home in Barford, Rose would deliver the rabbits to Fred's customers.

This way of life continued for many years after the war until the arrival of the disease, myxomatosis. It first arrived in the UK in September 1953 and by 1955 around 95% of the country's rabbits had been wiped out. Fred describes how, almost overnight, he went from seeing thousands of rabbits to seeing none.

There were a few that survived, but you couldn't find them. Nobody wanted to buy and eat one anyway. Funny thing was that, around Ivers, it was the last place myxi hit, there were loads of foxes and stoats and weasels. At night it was all foxes because they were after the dead and dying rabbits. Everywhere else the rabbits had gone! They'd all lived on rabbits. After that you didn't see a stoat for a very long time, didn't get them in traps. I did kill a lot of foxes that year. So after that I had to do more keepering.

Fred spent more of his time controlling vermin and rearing a small number of pheasants, but keepering was still part-time with the rest of his time spent working on the farm. At harvest time he could just as easily be found driving a combine harvester as in a field rearing a few pheasants. Fred's life changed in other ways too, as in June 1953 his daughter, Marion, was born. Queen Elizabeth's coronation was on 2nd June and poor Rose had to miss the village celebrations as she waddled around with her very large bump. Their daughter arrived eight days later on the tenth. In 1958, with the prospect of a larger wage packet, Fred moved to a full-time gamekeeper position on Hurdcott Estate.

Chapter 2

Hurdcott Estate is just a mile or so west of Barford St Martin. The River Nadder flows through the middle of the estate and is exactly how you would imagine a chalk stream to be. To the side of Hurdcott House is a large manmade lake. Either side of the river meadows the land rises with rolling farmland and woods, rising into high down land at its southern borders. On its eastern side is the boundary with the farm Fred had worked on since the late 1930s.

When Fred arrived on the estate there were two decaying horseboxes in a field by the large wood. These were the last remnants of a time when the estate and its then owner, Captain Forester, were involved in one of the largest horse racing gambling coups of all time. In 1903, Captain Forester was part of the Druids Lodge Confederacy, also known as The Hermits of Salisbury Plain, which owned and raced horses out of stables at Druids Lodge. In 1903, the Confederacy began racing a horse called Hackler's Pride, trained by Jack Fallon. They raced the horse in The Cambridgeshire at Newmarket, and also involved three other seemingly better horses to confuse the bookmakers. Hackler's Pride was given odds of 25-1. As a result of their scheming, Hackler's pride won The Cambridgeshire easily, netting the Confederacy £200,000, equivalent to ten million pounds today.

During World War I, Hurdcott had been home to Australian

soldiers and, high on the downs overlooking the estate, was a large map of Australia carved into the chalk. One of Fred's standard jokes was to say to his children that he had just walked across Australia. Sadly, this large chalk map has now disappeared under grass, but the memories of other British and Commonwealth regiments that inhabited the fields for miles around live on in The Fovant Badges. This is now a tourist attraction for those driving along the A30.

When Fred went to Hurdcott Estate, his lifestyle improved considerably. The house they moved to was much larger than their house in Barford and it had the luxury of a fitted bathroom with flushing toilet and hot running water. The days of cold trips to the outhouse, potties under the bed and the outside water pump were gone. Fred benefited from better pay and of course there were tips, mainly at Christmas, which boosted his salary. With his improved salary, Fred was able to buy his first car, a Morris 8. He also got about half a ton of potatoes off the farm and as many logs for the fire as he wanted.

Fred went to Hurdcott Estate in the employ of a Mr Allen. The shoot had been neglected and there were a lot of vermin all over the estate; mostly foxes, badgers, jays and rats. Mr Allen was a keen shooting man and wanted the estate brought back to being a good shoot to entertain his friends, mainly business people such as George Usher the brewer, Mr Hoover, the maker of domestic appliances, and Arthur Street, the writer and broadcaster.

In his first year, Fred killed a lot of vermin. It was also a really good year for wild pheasants and the rearing went well, resulting in plenty of pheasants. Fred fed the lake and the rivers for ducks and developed a good duck shoot, killing about 100 ducks in a day. It was all going well and then, after the first year, Mr Allen died and the estate was put up for sale. That year, Fred decided to rear his pheasants in Rookery Field near his house rather than in the park as this was where all the estate's farm machinery was on view for the sale and Fred knew that all the people viewing it would be a problem for him and his hens. Throughout that summer there were a couple of sales of goods and Mr Walker Munro eventually bought the estate. He was a younger man without any real experience of shooting; however, he was keen and the shoot carried on in much the same way as before.

As is often the case when a new owner takes up residence, Mr Walker Munro decided to undertake some major work on the house. In order to do this he employed workmen who came from London. Like a lot of Londoners, they enjoyed an eel or two. By the house was a large eel trap, which regularly had 20 to 30 eels swimming in about a foot of water. The workmen asked Fred if they could have some. Fred didn't like handling eels so he told them they could have as many as they could catch. Eagerly, two of the workmen took off their shoes and socks and jumped in. Fred enjoyed the spectacle of the men hollering and leaping in and out of the trap as the eels slipped and slid over their bare feet. Needless to say, they didn't catch any.

After a while, Fred sent his dog, Bella, to catch one. She soon returned with one squirming around her nose. So the Londoners had their eel. Bella also caught eels for Fred's family to eat. As Fred didn't like to handle them it was Fred's son Derek's job to dispatch and skin them. This he did first by banging them on the head to kill them, then he would nail them through their heads to the apple tree in the garden. It was then a quick job to cut the skin around the neck and with a steady, but firm, grip pull downwards to strip the skin off.

Bella was the first of many dogs owned by Fred. He was a good dog handler and trainer and soon gained a reputation for how well his dogs worked. The estate was also gifted a Labrador dog by one of the guest guns, Lord Northess, who was associated with Crufts. This dog, Josie, was passed on to Fred. From Josie, Fred bred a litter of puppies; one yellow and five black. Fred also had Jack Russell terriers, which were used for bolting foxes and rat-catching. One of the first was a little character called Patchy. She had very short legs, which made her perfect for going down foxholes. What she lacked in stature she made up for in courage. On one occasion she appeared out of a fox's hole with the fox's tail in her mouth! Bella was quite protective towards Patchy, especially if Patchy wanted a swim in the river. No sooner had she jumped in than Bella would follow and 'retrieve' her.

Hurdcott was overrun with vermin when Fred arrived. He used mainly traps and wires and poison to kill rats. Vermin were a constant headache and, although they would be caught all year round, it was in the early months of the year that Fred had more time to set his traps and wires. He caught mainly foxes and it was not unusual to catch up to 30 badgers a year. As a result of the reduction in numbers of badgers and foxes came an increase in game birds and also an increase in songbirds. Vermin are not choosy which nests they raid or which birds they kill. In the

1950s and 60s, animal skins could be sold for a small sum. So when badgers and foxes were caught they were skinned. Rose would wrap the skins up and take them to the Post Office to send to Harries Friend of Wisbech, Cambridgeshire. As well as the skins, Rose would also send squirrel tails, pheasant tail feathers and jay wings. The skins and tails would be used in clothing and the feathers for adorning women's and men's hats. Badger hair was used in the manufacture of gentlemen's shaving brushes. A few days after posting, Fred would receive a Postal Order for a few shillings as payment. With smaller vermin like weasels and crows, Fred carried on the old tradition of hanging the corpses on barbed wire fences. In some parts of the country this is called a gamekeeper's larder.

In February, Fred would start to catch live adult pheasants for breeding. Fred used two methods for catching adult pheasants. The first was a homemade trap made of willow that looked a little like a large beehive when it was constructed. Propping it up with two sticks set the trap. One stick was bent to form a hoop. The hoop was placed on the ground and the other stick held up the trap. Grain was put inside to attract the pheasants and when they entered the trap and trod on the hoop it knocked the stick out and the trap fell over the pheasant. The other method was a bit more productive. A ten-feet by six-feet pen was constructed with a funnel at one end. Grain for food was put in the pen for a day or two; the pheasants would enter via the funnel and not be able to get out again. This method caught 20 to 30 pheasants at a time. When the pheasants had been caught, Fred would swap some of the cock pheasants with neighbouring shoots in order to mix the gene pool.

When the pheasant had been caught they had to have one of their wings tied up in order that they did not fly out of the aviaries they would end up in. Fred did this using a piece of 22-inch-long black tape. Some gamekeepers used leather brails made for the purpose, but Fred preferred his tried and tested method. The tape was kinder to the pheasants as it had more give in it than the brails. The tape was tied around the thickest part of the wing and when the pheasants were released it was easy just to cut it off.

The pheasants were put into a large aviary near Fred's house. There was plenty of room for them to run around and Fred put in bales of straw and branches to provide cover for laying. There would be seven hen pheasants to one cock pheasant. Fred would start feeding these pheasants with laying pellets in order to get better quality eggs. The first eggs usually appeared in the last week of March and were collected and eaten by the family; it was a spring treat to have two fried pheasant eggs for breakfast! From 1st to 14th April the eggs were collected and sold to other estates or game farms and after the 14th the eggs were kept. The eggs were collected twice a day for Rose to wash and sort. Any eggs that were abnormal in any way – too small or too big, with soft or cracked shells – were kept for eating whilst the others were put for hatching.

At this time Fred would also get his hencoops and pens ready. Fred raised the pheasants in the park. To try to reduce diseases, a different spot was chosen each year. The coops would be creosoted and arranged in rows and the pens put up and made secure. Fred also had an old shepherd hut that he used to keep all the feed and other bits and pieces he might need. It also provided a shady spot for his dogs on hot sunny days. One year, Fred chose a spot under a tree for the sitting boxes. One day a branch fell off and smashed the sitting boxes underneath.

During the latter part of April, Fred would visit all the local farms and houses where he could buy broody hens. This was often an evening job as he took along his daughter, Marion, to help. The Land Rover would be loaded up with wooden crates and they would set off to places like Barford, Burcombe, Dinton, Compton Chamberlain and as far as Old Sarum to buy the hens. When they had enough they would take them home and Fred would sit the hens in the coops. The first broody hens would be sat on 1st May.

Each hen would be given 20 eggs. A pheasant egg takes between 23 and 25 days to hatch, so during this time each hen had to be taken off the eggs for a short period of time to eat and drink. Fred would sit 90 hens. Each had a piece of cord with a loop on it tied to one of their legs. Outside each sitting box was a small stake, and when the hen was feeding the loop of cord went over the stake so the hen would not wander away. Fred was thus able to ensure that each hen was put back on the right eggs. Fred managed his 90 hens by taking each hen off the nest one at a time. By the time he got to the last hen, it was time to put the first one he had removed back onto her eggs. When the eggs hatched, the hen and her brood of chicks were moved to a new coop with a pen attached. They would stay in these coops and runs for six weeks.

Water and feed was put into separate metal feeders. These had to be kept clean, again to keep diseases at bay. This was not foolproof. A common complaint suffered by pheasants was gapeworm. This is quite a common problem for game birds and chickens. Eating the worm's eggs, which have either been coughed up by other infested birds or carried on hosts such as snails and slugs, causes an infestation of gapeworm. Gapeworm can be easily recognised as the birds gasp for breath, cough and often stretch their necks or shake their heads. If it is left untreated, the pheasants will eventually die. In the early days, treatment was given by shutting the infected pheasants into a coop and blowing in a white powder. This made the pheasant cough and expel the gapeworm. In later years the treatment was given in liquid form in drinking water, and now the treatment is added to the pheasants' food so that gapeworm is hardly seen.

After six weeks, the young pheasants were put into release pens in the woods. The pheasants were fed in the pens for a week or so but could find their own way out by flying over the wire, getting back in through wire funnels in the side of the pens. Fred kept some of the broody hens for himself, some went to the estate gardener, who kept chickens for the 'big house', and others were sold on. Fred's focus then turned to trying to keep his pheasants on the estate. This was done by regularly putting down feed in the woods and through September and October beating the boundaries of the estate and using his dogs to round up the pheasants and chase them back onto the estate.

All the sitting boxes had to be dismantled and stored and the feeders and drinkers thoroughly washed and disinfected for the following year.

Duck shooting was also an important feature at Hurdcott. From August onwards, Fred would start to feed the lake and two ponds under the woods. Hundreds of wild ducks would take up residence. The estate had a couple of duck shoots before the pheasant-shooting season started. Duck shoots only took place in the morning and often resulted in bags of 100 or more ducks. The guns would walk from the main house to their positions while Fred would walk to the other side of the lake and put the ducks up. This usually worked very well; however, there was one occasion where things went wrong. The guns left the house to walk to their positions and Fred set off to his side of the lake. There was only one spot where Fred could see the guns; this was as they walked over the bridge. Fred waited to see that they all crossed the bridge and then proceeded to his side of the lake and put the ducks up. However, there were no shots!

Fred couldn't work out what had happened so walked alongside the lake towards where the guns should have been. As he went a few ducks took flight, followed by the odd shot at them. When Fred finally caught up with the guns he discovered what had happened. One of the guns, after crossing the bridge, had discovered he had left his cartridge bag behind in the house. All the guns went back to the house with him to fetch it. There was no way of Fred knowing this, so he had put the ducks up! When the guns realised this, they had run back as fast as they could to their positions. But it was too late and most of the ducks had gone. Needless to say, it was a very poor bag that day.

The first pheasant shoot was at the end of October and the shoots went on throughout the winter until the season ended on 1st February. The biggest and most important shoots took place throughout November and December. The early shoots would take place around the outside perimeters of the estate and on these days there would be a bag of around 100 birds. On the 'good' days, utilising the woods in the middle of the estate, the bag contained around 200 pheasants and occasionally other birds such as the odd partridge and snipe. On an average day there would be four drives in the morning and three in the afternoon. The shoot employed between ten and 12 beaters on the shooting days. These were casual workers who came for both the love of shooting and being in the countryside and to earn a few extra shillings. They came from all walks of life and, at Hurdcott, many were policemen.

In the week before the shoot, Fred would go out with numbered stakes and place them in the fields. These stakes marked the spot where the guns had to stand. Fred also had to hire his beaters, although most of them came for every shoot during a season. He also had to organise two 'pickers-up'. These were people who had dogs that would retrieve the pheasants that had been shot and hunt for any that might have been wounded. The beaters would form a line at the edge of a wood, or a field with cover such as kale. When Fred gave the signal, usually by blowing a whistle, they would all walk forward, staying in line, and driving any pheasants before them. When the pheasants got to the end of the cover they would fly and the guns could shoot them. This is not easy; it takes a good shot to down a pheasant. On one occasion, one of the guns, Lord Jellico, who at the time was the First Sea Lord, managed to shoot a particularly high bird. It was a very good shot and he turned to Fred, delighted at his exploits, saying, '*I shot him with a sea slug missile, Fred.*'

Shoots were often eventful, but not always for the right reasons. Beaters travelled between the drives on the back of an open trailer towed by a tractor. These trailers were often crowded with the 12 beaters, Fred with his dogs and sometimes the pickers-up with their dogs. On one occasion, Fred's dog fell off the trailer, went under its wheel and was killed. This was very sad and upset the family for weeks.

Shoots can attract onlookers. This is dangerous, as nobody involved in the shoot knows the person is there. This happened on one shoot where a local boy, Bobby Rickets, looked over a hedge just as a gun fired his shotgun towards him. Bobby was peppered with shot and had to be rushed to hospital. Thankfully, he was not seriously hurt and survived to tell the tale. Fred had to deal with the aftermath, talking to the boy's parents and dealing with the ensuing police investigation. That evening, he went to the big house to report to Mr Walker Munro on the boy's condition and conversation he had with the boy's parents. It had been very traumatic for all concerned. Fred was handed a large glass of strong alcohol by his employer. It was so strong that Fred was quite inebriated when he left, and found himself staggering back up the road to his house. From that day on, for the rest of his working life, Fred never had a drink in the company of his boss again.

On another occasion, Fred walked over the top of a hill at Barford and came across another gamekeeper, Tommy Steel, who was busy taking his trousers down! Fred asked him what on earth he was doing and was told, '*The bugger shot me in the arse!*' Indeed, his backside was peppered with shot. Tommy had seen the gun was about to fire and had turned his back on him, thus getting the pellets in his backside rather than in his midriff. It did cause some hilarity but was not really a laughing matter.

There were none at Hurdcott, but Fred did go on organised deer shoots on other estates. Deer shooting was particularly dangerous, so on these days it was usually other gamekeepers and experienced shots that were asked to go. These shoots were mainly in Grovely and Big Ridge. Each wood was shot for deer on two occasions and on each day about 30 deer were shot with 12 bore shotguns, using big shot such as SSGs or AAA cartridges. Occasionally, Fred would shoot a deer on Hurdcott for himself. Then he would bring it to the house and hang it up by its back legs on the apple tree. This ensures all the blood runs into the head and does not congeal in the body, spoiling the meat. Fred would skin the animal and remove its internal organs. The liver and heart were kept for eating. The carcass was then taken into the kitchen where Fred would cut joints of meat, using a hacksaw to cut through the bone. The venison would be divided out between the family and other workers on the estate. It was Rose's unenviable job to clean up the mess in the kitchen when they had finished. The deer skin and innards were buried deep out in the woods so that foxes wouldn't dig it up again.

In 1963, Fred had to deal with the coldest winter since 1740. Snow started falling on Boxing Day and got up to 30cm deep. It remained on the ground until March. There were large snowdrifts, the roads and railways were blocked, and telephone lines were brought down. The hamlet on the estate where Fred lived was cut off and nothing could move around the estate for days. Some parts of the land were not visited during the whole winter. All shoots were cancelled and all Fred could do was feed the pheasants in some of the woods where he could get access. Fred caught his breeding pheasants early as he thought they would be difficult to catch when the snow eventually thawed. He put them in the bedrooms of the old gamekeeper's house, which was in the middle of the woods. They stayed in these rooms for two months and nobody else knew they were there.

Fred concentrated his efforts on just keeping his family safe and well. The children did not go to school for a couple of weeks as the school was frozen up and it was impossible for the school bus to get around its route. When the roads were not blocked they were extremely icy, and on three separate occasions Fred span the Land Rover around, luckily not touching the bank. The Watts family also lived in the hamlet where Fred lived and during this time one of their children got measles. They needed to get to the doctor at Fovant to collect some medicine. Fred was the only person with a Land Rover so was asked if he could take the father. This was a distance of about four miles on the A30. On the journey they had to dig the vehicle out of the snow on no fewer than three occasions.

It was very difficult to get about and nothing could get on to the estate. The baker left food at the end of the drive and somebody would collect it and distribute the supplies around the families on the farm.. The problems were on such a large scale that the authorities offered no help to rural communities, so Fred and his family were left to sort out any problems for themselves.

Burcombe, around 1917/18. House where Fred was born and grew up on left, his mother and father are first two figures on left.

Fred (age 21) and Rosemary (age 17) on their wedding day. Ansty, 6th Oct, 1946.

Fred's mother, Ann (Granny Kellow), outside cottage where Fred was born, 1920s.

Pheasants in Hurdcott wood showing pens and coops, 1958–1968.

Fred at Hurdcott with dogs Trixie and Bella, around 1958/9.

Marion with dogs Trixie, Bella and Josie. Hurdcott, winter of 1963.

Rose with Trixie outside their cottage, The Rookery at Hurdcott, winter of 1963.

Fred's tractor by the Pheasant Aviary. Temple Valley, Matterley Estate, 1970s.

Rose with the puppies. Hurdcott around 1963/4.

Fred looking at his pheasant eggs in the incubator. Matterley Estate, 1970s.

Pheasants in pens, about 4 weeks old. Matterley, 1970s–1988.

The first hatching – pheasant chicks in incubator. 1970s/80s.

Fred by pheasant rearing pens.
Temple Valley, Matterley, 1970s.

'Pop' in back garden of house.
Fred's rearing pens in background.
Temple Valley, 1980s.

Fred with Jilly the dog by his rearing pens, 1980s.

Young pheasants about 5 weeks old.

Rose and Nigel (one of the 'boys') in back garden at Temple Valley. In the background the old railway carriages and shed used as game larders in the shooting season, 1980s.

Fred outside the Brooder House (carrying a water feeder), 1970s.

Rose and Fred on holiday in Cyprus, early 1980s.

Counting 'The Bag' after a shoot. Front: Frank Pierce (gamekeeper on neighbouring estate) behind, Frank's 'boy' and Alan Osmond, Matterley 1970s/80s.

The guns on a keeper's shoot. Fred: front row-centre in black coat and wearing trilby; behind, Lt Cm Bruce. Front row, second on left: Derek, Fred's son. 1980s, Temple Valley Farm, Matterley Estate.

After Fred retired. Lt Cm Bruce and Fred on a shoot at Matterley, 1990s/2000s.

Fred with Teal and Crumble, picking up on a day's shoot at Matterley, 1990s/2000s.

Enjoying retirement, Fred fishing at Langford, 2000s.

Fred didn't have a lot of trouble from poachers. There were two local men, Mr Hilliard and Mr Wiltshire, from Barford St Martin who were caught poaching a few times. However, Fred did have plenty of other incidents to deal with. One morning, Fred was feeding his pheasants in the wood when a man appeared, saying he was taking a shortcut. Fred knew he came from what was later to be known as Guys Marsh Prison near Shaftsbury. He told the man to come with him, making the man walk in front so that he would not get attacked from behind. As soon as they reached the Park the man ran off, streaking across the field towards Barford. Fred ran the other way and phoned the police. The police in Barford picked up the escaped prisoner later in the day. There was a very similar incident on another occasion. Fred was with another gamekeeper, Earny Camel from Compton Chamberlain, when they saw another escaped prisoner at Barford Hollow. Again, this was reported to the police and the man was arrested in Barford.

In the 1960s, Fred was caught up in a manhunt for an escaped prisoner from Dartmoor Prison, who was known to be dangerous. A day or so after the escape a man was seen early in the morning, changing his boots. When challenged, he ran off into Hurdcott woods. The police immediately got in touch with Fred and asked him to help them in their search. At first Fred refused, as he was afraid for the safety of his family and wanted to stay at home and watch over them. The police were also concerned because Fred had his guns in the house. The police sent a dog handler to guard the houses and the children, and the local policeman called at the house and collected Fred's guns. Fred then went out with a large contingent of policemen and soldiers to search the woods and outbuildings. Rose and her neighbour were working at the big house and the police came and searched through the house. Roadblocks were set up in Barford and in the surrounding area. It was a very worrying time, as the escaped prisoner was known to be a very dangerous man.

Fred also had to deal with other incidents involving the army. On one occasion an army helicopter flew into high-tension electricity wires and crashed, killing the pilot. Fred gave them access to the site as they carried out their investigations and removed the crashed helicopter. One morning, Fred came across an army armoured car coming up the drive to Hurdcott House. Fred met them by the front gate and the soldier in charge said he intended to park there. Fred said, '*You bloody ain't!*' They said they were going to park there all day. Fred told them it was not an army place and they had to go. The soldier said he would get in touch with his commanding officer and Fred said, '*Of course you will, and tell him I'm here and you ain't stopping!*' So they drove off.

Mr Walker Munro was a young man when he bought Hurdcott and Fred enjoyed working for him. After seven years, however, Mr Munro became seriously ill and died. His widow desperately wanted to run the shoot as it had always been run. However, it became obvious to Fred that this was not going to work for him. The farm manager was not interested in the shoot, so Fred could not get the support and cooperation he needed to continue. So Fred started to look for pastures new and soon found a new position as gamekeeper to Commander Henry Bruce, of Matterley Estate near Winchester.

Chapter 3

Matterley Estate is situated on the south side of the A31 between Winchester and Alresford in Hampshire. It is approximately 1,800 acres and lies across five picturesque valleys with the highest point at Cheesefoot Head at 175m above sea level. From these high points there are magnificent views across the countryside and on a clear day the sea is clearly visible. The estate lies within the South Downs, and the South Down Way went past Fred's front gate. The landscape is quite dramatic in places, particularly the Punch Bowl. The steep sides of the Punch Bowl are colonised by a number of rare and important orchids, chalk land grasses and butterflies. In June 1944, prior to D-Day, the Punch Bowl was used as the venue for General Eisenhower to address up to 100,000 American troops. In one corner of the bowl, Joe Louis, the World Heavyweight boxer, gave exhibition bouts to entertain the soldiers. When Fred arrived on the estate the sides of the Punchbowl were used by a flock of sheep or cattle and the bowl floor was cultivated to grow corn. On the north side of the estate runs the A31 and some of the land north of the road was owned by Commander Bruce's father. It consisted mainly of Hampage Wood, in the middle of which was the Gospel Oak. This was an ancient oak tree surrounded by iron railings. Local folklore says the Gospel Oak was the only remaining oak tree in the wood after the rest were taken in the 12th century to build Winchester

Cathedral. Hampage Wood also had wide-open rides, which provided attractive routes through the woodland. There were also some large areas of woodland on the main estate – Great Clump, Blackbushes, and French's – and belts of trees and bushes that had been planted to provide cover for pheasants.

Fred had his interview for the job at Matterley in October 1966. It was the only job he ever formally applied for. He received the princely sum of £2 10s 0d for his travelling expenses from Hurdcott to Matterley. Fred was offered the job immediately and took up his new role on Saturday 4th February 1967. His new job came with a number of perks and better pay, which were spelled out in the following way:

Matterley Estate Terms of Employment

It is hoped to commence employment on Saturday 4th February, 1967.

Wages – will be £13. 10s. 0d per week.

Dog money – ten shillings per week.

Free house during employment on the estate.

Repairs to cottage – the estate will carry out all outside and structural repairs and supply materials for inside decoration.

One ton of logs supplied free each autumn.

Suit of clothes supplied free each July, not exceeding £20.

12 days' holiday with pay each year, or pay in lieu.

One month's notice on either side.

Milk – two pints free each day.

Bonus

One shilling each for every cock pheasant shot, up to the first 500 in any one year.

Partridges: 1/6d

Two shillings will be paid for each cock pheasant shot after the first 500 in any one year.

In addition to the above, Fred was also given a car for his sole use on the estate and for personal use, as well as petrol from the farm's pumps. He also had a telephone, enough bags of potatoes to last each winter and was given a turkey at Christmas. There were of course other benefits; tips from the guns on each shoot and the general benefits of living off the land. This all amounted to a great improvement in living conditions for Fred and the family.

The move also came with some other changes. Derek, Fred's son, was working himself by this time so he did not move with the family. Instead, he went to live with Rose's parents in Teffont. When the family moved into the cottage at Temple Valley there were just Fred, Rose and their daughter Marion, who by this time was 13 years old.

The house was situated in the middle of the estate and surrounded on two sides by woodland, with magnificent views over the chalk hills and valleys. There were no other houses but there was a farmyard and the public footpath, the South Down Way, went past the front gate. This meant that the general public were always about somewhere, from soldiers from the Winchester Barracks doing training runs, to contingents of the Sealed Knot Society on route marches, to ramblers and horse riders. Over the next 20 years there were many hundreds of encounters with wayfarers, walking or running or riding past the front gate. Winchester was about three miles to the west and Alresford two miles to the east of the estate. The nearest villages, Ovington and Avington, were also two to three miles away.

Next to the house on one side were three large aviaries where Fred penned his pheasants in the spring. On the other side was a large brooder house, with outside pens and an incubator house. This was another big change as Fred moved from hatching eggs with broody hens to using incubators. However, old habits die hard and Fred carried on using some broody hens for the first few years.

Commander Bruce was a very keen shooting man, but when Fred arrived the shoot turned out to be quite neglected and the bags very small. A great deal of money had been spent on the shoot for not a great deal of return. The estate was overrun with vermin and the pheasants were tiny. In the first few years Fred had to spend quite some time killing foxes, badgers and other vermin in order to get on top of the situation. He also had to improve his pheasant stock by swapping pheasants with other estates to improve the bloodline; this gradually improved the quality of the birds he was able to produce.

Matterley was a much bigger shoot than Hurdcott and each year Fred bred about 3,000 pheasants. This required a different breeding system, so Fred had incubators for hatching the eggs and a brooder house for rearing them. However, the brooder house did not provide enough space for all the pheasants. Therefore, Fred erected small brooder houses and pens each summer in one of the fields near his house. This all took a great deal of work as each year the brooder house and pens would have to be cleaned and disinfected and often painted with creosote. He also had to put out all his heaters and ensure they were all clean and working. When the pens had been erected it was a constant battle to ensure they were secure and the pheasants could not escape. It was equally important to ensure that foxes, stoats, weasels and birds of prey could not get in!

Fred had three aviaries with adult pheasants laying the eggs. As before, he had to catch the pheasants and tie their wings. At the beginning of April he started to collect the eggs. Rose would wash and sort them, with Fred carrying out the final check, and every seven days he sat a shelf of eggs in the incubators. When the incubators were full there were 1,000 eggs in them. All the eggs had to be turned by pulling a lever which made the eggs roll over, and it was important to keep the temperature and humidity at the correct level. When the chicks started to hatch they were left in the incubators for the first few hours to dry off their feathers. From the end of April through May and June there were pheasants hatching each week. Each hatching comprised approximately 500 chicks. Before the shelf could be filled again it had to be cleaned and disinfected. The eggshells, unhatched eggs and mess from the hatching had to be disposed of. This was all necessary in order to ensure bacteria or viruses did not infect the chicks.

The hatched chicks were put carefully into a cardboard box and taken to the brooder house where the chicks were placed under a gas heater. A circle of cardboard was placed around the heater to ensure the chicks did not wander away from the heat. Here they remained for a few days, during which Fred would feed them with small rearing 'crumbs' to start with. As they got bigger the feed changed to pellets. After about a week the ring of cardboard was removed and the pheasant chicks were able to wander further afield. The chicks now knew where the heat was and would return if they got cold.

Before the pheasants were released they had to be 'debeaked'. This entailed cutting off the tip of the top beak; a painless and harmless procedure, albeit very time consuming. The top beak would regrow and sometimes 'debeaking' had to be done again. When a lot of pheasants are penned together they have a habit of pecking each other's feathers out, sometimes to the extent of being left completely bald on their backs. This can leave them to the mercy of the cold and wet weather, and many would die if left. 'Debeaking' is therefore a preventative measure.

On one occasion Fred was busy debeaking in one small brooder house in the field. The house had small stable doors and Fred had left the top door open to allow in light and air. His black Labrador dog kept coming and poking its head over the top of the door and whining. Fred sent it away in no uncertain terms, but the dog kept persisting. Eventually, Fred turned to see what was wrong and noticed the bottom door was slightly ajar and the chicks were escaping through the gap. Fearing he was going to lose them all, he went out to look for the escapees. There was his dog, lying on the ground, surrounded by pheasant chicks, with a look of '*I told you so!*' clearly written across her face.

When the pheasants were a week or two old they were

released into the big pens attached to the brooder house. Here they remained for a further four weeks. They had to be fed and watered twice a day and every night they had to be shut up back into the brooder house. Shutting in the pheasants often involved the whole family, and sometimes the dog! Pheasants are fairly stupid creatures and when faced with a tiny hole into a warm brooder house will try to turn back. They are also easily frightened and if you are not very careful will fly up and scatter. So shutting up the pheasants tried the patience, and involved a lot of creeping and quiet shushing. One of Fred's dogs, a Springer spaniel called Jilly, was brilliant at helping to shut in the pheasants. The usual format was Fred at the front, driving in the birds, Marion just behind to stop any escapees, and Jilly behind to capture any escaped birds. On many occasions she would retrieve a startled pheasant and give it to Fred without a single ruffled feather. Once a pheasant took to the air and was flying to the back of the pen when Jilly leapt from the ground, all four feet in the air, caught the pheasant in her jaws, landed and returned it to Fred. Apart from being very startled, the pheasant was completely unharmed without a mark on it.

In 1970 there was a national and very serious outbreak of fowl pest. This is a devastating disease that affects chickens, other types of fowl and game birds. It could have spelt disaster for the shoot. If the pheasants had become infected, all the birds would have either died of the disease or have to be slaughtered. Fowl pest is an airborne virus and some of the estates and farms around Matterley had it. There was therefore a very real and tangible threat for Fred that he could lose all his birds if it was discovered on the estate. The Farm

Agent acted for many of the local farms and visited them on at least a weekly basis. One of the Agent's jobs at Matterley was to bring Fred his wages each week. During the fowl pest outbreak, Fred told him not to come near his house or the pheasants for fear of spreading the virus. Therefore, Fred's wages were left at the boss's house and Fred would go and collect them. For Fred, the threat of fowl pest also meant he had to inject all his birds with a drug to prevent the pheasants catching it. All 3,000 birds had to be done, each individually. It was a very time-consuming job as first the birds had to be caught and injected, and the injected birds separated from those that had not been inoculated.

On many occasions, Fred's daughter, Marion, was called in to help. Each bird was caught with a net, removed and held while Fred inoculated each bird by its breastbone. When the bird wriggled and the injection gun slipped it was either Fred's or Marion's hand that got jabbed!

After six weeks the pheasant chicks would be taken to release pens in the woods. At Matterley there were a number of release pens, all in the bigger woods – Long Clump, Blackbushes, Round Clump, Southampton Clump and Hampage. Like the release pens at Hurdcott, these pens allowed the pheasants to fly out and get back in through wire funnels. The birds were fed daily on straw that Fred had previously scattered in and around the pens. Sometimes Marion would be called in to help, and once, as they were going through the woods, weaving through the trees with the tractor and trailer, Fred caught the edge of a bale on a tree and the whole lot came off with Marion on top!

As the shooting season drew near, Fred would take his dogs – the, Labradors and later a Springer Spaniel called Jilly – and beat the hedges on the boundary of the estate to drive the pheasants back on to the farm. The pheasant-shooting season starts on 1st October but the first shoots at Matterley were nearer the end of the month, always on Tuesdays. Hampage Wood was shot just four times during the season and some of these days were for Commander Bruce's father and later for his brother, Victor. During the week before the shoot, Fred and Commander Bruce would go to each drive and decide where the shooting pegs should go. On at least one occasion, as they were putting out the pegs, Commander Bruce expressed wryly, *'Doesn't matter where I put these Fred, does it? Because you'll come back and change them if you don't like where they are going.'*

This was very true; Fred usually had things his way. Each season, Fred also recruited his group of beaters. Most were serving policemen or firemen and included a local uniformed police sergeant and detective sergeant. The beaters usually came on a regular basis as they enjoyed their day in the country. Fred also had to ensure there were at least two pickers-up for each shoot. Sometimes these were friends of the boss, Mrs Harrison being one, and sometimes it was another gamekeeper. On the day of the shoot the guns met at the boss' house and drew lots for the first gun peg of the day. After that they moved along two pegs on each drive. The beaters met at the farm by Fred's house. When all were present they would set off for the first drive, to start around 9.30 a.m. The beaters, Fred and his gun dogs, and sometimes the pickers-up would go on a covered trailer with bales of straw for seating. On each drive the beaters would line up and at the given signal would move forward, driving the pheasants and anything else before them. They scrambled through bracken and thorns, climbed over fallen trees and fences, and beat through scrub and high kale. On wet days they got soaked through. The shoot carried on in most weathers. If the weather was particularly bad with rain, snow or fog, the day would be shortened by either starting a little later or finishing early. After the first few years, foxes were seldom seen on shooting days but on one day, a day when Prince Edward was a guest, up popped a fox and ran between His Royal Highness and the next gun! As Fred remarked at the time, '*It would be on that day of all days!*'

At the end of a day's shooting, all the guns would be give a brace (two) of pheasants to take home. This was Fred's opportunity to meet each gun and be given a tip for the day by each. The rest of the pheasants were put in the game larder. This was an old railway goods van, converted for the purpose. The pheasants were hung in twos on poles, which stretched across the width of the larder. Other game such as partridges, snipe or widgeon were also hung. This could be quite a messy job on a wet day. On one day Fred was helped by one of the guest guns, who asked Fred if there was somewhere he could wash his hands. Fred pointed him towards the house and the kitchen. Rose had just washed the floor! The gentleman entered and walked to the sink, still wearing his muddy boots, and proceeded to wash his hands with his back to the door. Rose was not pleased to see her floor messed up again and exclaimed, '*I am fed up with you lot coming in here with your bloody muddy boots on!'* The gentleman turned, apologised and left, telling Fred on the way out that he had upset Rose. Fred went back in the house, laughing and said, *'Do you know who you have just told off? Only the Duke of Luxembourg!'*

All the game was sold to a game dealer. Fred would negotiate a price for the pheasants for the season. At this time, pheasants were selling for £6 a brace early in the season and £4 a brace after Christmas. In the early years, most of the pheasants were exported to the French market, but in later years they went mainly to London. Fred used the same dealers to sell rabbits, hares and deer.

Gradually, Fred's efforts paid off and the shoot improved year on year. After five years the bags had improved considerably. The summer of 1975 was very hot and dry. All Fred's pheasants did well and he lost very few that he bred. Wild pheasants also bred well that year and reared more chicks than usual. That winter, the shoot had its best year ever, the bag increasing to double the size of earlier years. From then on, Fred worked hard each year to keep this standard up until he retired many years later. The best days shooting regularly had bags of 500 to 600 birds; the record was 661.

Each year at Matterley they shot approximately the same number of pheasants reared. This caused some consternation amongst the neighbouring estates, which jumped to the conclusion that Fred must attract pheasants from other shoots in order to achieve the bags he did. So, one year, Fred bred some pure white pheasants. These were quite a novelty and, of course, some wandered onto other estates, thus proving that Fred lost some pheasants across the boundaries too! One keeper even contacted Fred to say that he had caught a white cock pheasant and asked if Fred could give him a white hen so he could breed from them. Fred gave a quick and short reply: '*No, you give the cock back, the bugger's mine!*'

In late August, after the corn had been cut, Fred and a few others would go rabbit shooting. This happened at nighttime. Fred always drove the Land Rover and there would be two or three others who would do the shooting. Derek, Fred's son, often came, sometimes the 'boy' who was working for Fred, and sometimes another gamekeeper. They would go out as it was getting dark and stay out until about 11 o'clock at night. Rabbits and the occasional hare were caught in the Land Rover's headlights. Each night they got about 40 rabbits. Fred would sell most of these and pocket the money for himself; an additional perk of the job. After the shoot, the men would come back to the house and have a late supper before heading home.

Another visitor to the estate was Mr Geelong. He was a wealthy Belgian aristocrat who spent his time travelling the world, hunting. When he came to Matterley he was interested in deer, but only the stags. He was particularly keen to get any stags that had a good set of antlers to keep as a trophy. His efforts also helped to cull the deer. Fred's job was to find him the deer and Mr Geelong was left to do the hunting. Later in the evening Mr Geelong would bring any shot deer to the house to be hung in the game larder. The venison was sold to a game dealer, but the heads were kept. Fred would skin the head and saw the skull in half, leaving the forehead and nose attached to the antlers. Rose had the unenviable job of boiling the antlers and bones. When this had been done, any flesh was scraped off and the head left to dry. The smell when this was being done was horrible. Mr Geelong would collect his trophies at the end of the week and leave Fred with a good tip. He was a very amiable man and often when he brought the deer to the house he would come into the cottage and sit by the fire in his stocking feet. He enjoyed a cup of tea and bite to eat and a good chat with Fred and the family. He often swapped stories of his hunting exploits, particularly hunting wild boar on his estate in Belgium.

Chapter 4

At Hurdcott, Fred did not have many problems with poachers. Matterley was a different story; there were problems with poachers and hare coursers all the time. Fred believed that some of this was due to the close proximity of the big cities of Portsmouth and Southampton. Indeed, he believed that some of the hare coursing was due to men training their greyhounds for the dog track in Portsmouth. The estate was also fairly remote as there were only a small number of farm cottages scattered across the fields and woodland. It was easy therefore to hide, or it would have been if Fred did not have a good ear and a good understanding of when and where poachers would turn up.

The hare coursers usually came on Sunday mornings, and most of them were Travellers. Sometimes, a number would come together on what amounted to an organised meet, and other times they would come on their own. When Fred caught them there were usually polite exchanges at first, the perpetrators calling Fred 'Sir'. However, as soon as Fred said, '*You're nicked!*' the attitude changed and Fred was then referred to as '*You bastard!*' One chap came flying at Fred with fists up, shouting '*I'm Irish.*' This didn't faze Fred at all. He immediately put his own fists up and retorted, '*I'm Hampshire!*' His assailant quickly calmed down when he realised that Fred was made of stern stuff and would not be intimidated.

After a few years the estate invested in an anti-poaching alarm system. This was a forerunner of the CCTV systems that are common today. The main woods were set up with this system. It consisted of very long air-filled pipes, which were laid across tracks and gateways and worked when somebody stepped on a pipe. The pipes were laid back across the estate to Fred's house. In the house was a large alarm box with numbered lights and a loud alarm. When a pipe was stood on, the corresponding light would flash and the alarm sounded. Fred therefore knew in which wood or part of the wood the alarm had been triggered. When this system was working well it was very effective. One night, Fred had gone to a local pub for a well-earned pint or two. Back at the house the alarm sounded. Rose rang the pub and told Fred which number light had been activated. Fred left the pub and went straight to the relevant wood and caught his poacher.

The system did have many problems though. Animals such as deer could set it off, and tractors driving over a pipe would easily break it. So from time to time Fred still used one of the old methods of detection; an alarm gun. This was a contraption set up with a blank cartridge and a wire stretching across a track. When the wire was tripped the cartridge would go off with a loud bang, made even louder as it was set in an old metal milk churn! This also served to keep the cartridge dry. The noise would alert Fred and frighten the poacher.

At night time, if the alarm sounded, Fred would go to where he knew the poacher would have left a car. Before he left the house he would ring the police and sometimes a fellow gamekeeper in order to get some help. When Fred found the poacher's car he would hide. When the poachers returned, Fred would wait until they were astride the fence and then turn his torch on them. This usually had the result of the poacher falling off the fence; sometimes they ran away. They always had to come back to their car though, and by the time they returned the police would be there and the poacher arrested. These cases would then go to Court. Fred got a £40 bonus for every night poacher prosecuted. As Fred wryly said, *'If you got him just as the sun was going down, you hung on to him until it got dark!'*

Poachers also turned up in the daytime. When Fred was out one day he saw a man with a shotgun. Fred walked over and stood beside him as the man raised the gun and shot at a pheasant. He then turned to Fred and said, *'It's all right, I'm a gamekeeper.'* Fred's retort was, 'Bloody *bad luck, so am I.'* When the poacher went to Court, Fred was asked to repeat this conversation, much to the amusement of everybody present.

Another daytime poaching case caused some hilarity when it went to Court. Fred had caught the poacher about a quarter of a mile from his car, carrying a shotgun. In Court the poacher claimed he was just going for a pee. The Clerk to the Court asked, *'Do you always take a shotgun when you go for a pee?'* The whole Court burst out laughing.

Fred also caught a hare courser red handed, who tried to wriggle out of it by claiming he wasn't coursing hares, but trying to catch a fox. What he didn't know – and everybody else did – was that the sitting Magistrate was also the Master of the local foxhounds! Again, there was laughter in Court.

Fred went to Court for poaching cases almost on a monthly

basis, but not all cases were worth prosecuting. Fred caught some men rabbiting with ferrets. He agreed with the policeman that it wasn't worth prosecuting, so a little summary justice was meted out instead. The policeman asked for the car to be inspected to see if it was legal and the men could drive it. The men were caught in the early hours of the morning and they had to wait until the afternoon for the police inspection team to arrive and check their car. It was a long wait. That was their punishment.

Poaching wasn't the only problem Fred had to deal with. At weekends he would often come across courting couples in compromising positions! These were left alone though. Sometimes he had to deal with walkers who had gone off the footpaths and were trespassing. Often they had dogs or children that they allowed to run around in the woods or fields, totally oblivious to the damage they were causing. If they were contrite and apologetic, Fred would show them the quickest way to get back to their cars, but if they were stroppy he would often make them go on a long walk.

One night, Fred had just returned from the pub when he heard a lorry go past the house. This was a farm track and didn't lead to any roads, so immediately Fred deduced they were up to no good. There had been an incident before when overnight a large crop of swedes had been stolen. So a lorry going past the house at 11 o'clock at night was very suspicious. Fred called the police and then put his car across the farm track so the lorry could not get away. When the police arrived they went off in search of the lorry. Instead of finding a gang of poachers or thieves, they found the army! They were setting up a radio station! Again, there were a few sharp exchanges before the army packed up and left.

Occasionally, Fred would be woken in the middle of the night. Sometimes it was the poaching alarm and he would have to go out to investigate. Once it was the farm manager, as a herd of cows had got out on to the dual carriageway and all hands were needed to round them up. Somebody leaving the gate open had caused this. Another incident occurred when at about 1.30 a.m. there was a loud knocking on the door. Fred stuck his head out the window and saw a policeman there. A lady had hit a deer with her car and it had run into some cemetery railings and got its head stuck. They wanted Fred to go and dispatch the deer. He grabbed his gun and, after the deed was done, brought the deer back and hung it in the game larder. Later the following day the policemen turned up, looking for their bit of venison! It was how things worked then.

Chapter 5

In 1971 there was another big change for Fred and the family. In the September, Marion left home to go to Teacher Training College. Fred and Rose were on their own for the first time since their marriage in 1946. This newfound freedom led to them planning a holiday for the first time in all those long years, and in the March of 1972 they jetted off to Benidorm. They thoroughly enjoyed their first trip abroad and it was the first of many holidays to come. From then on, Fred took an annual two-week holiday each March.

The time together on their own was short-lived, as around this time Rose's elderly parents came to live with them. Rose's mother had suffered a stroke and also had chronic arthritis in her knees. Rose's father was finding it very difficult to cope, leading to Rose spending several days a week staying with them. It was decided that it would be better for all if the old folks moved from their house in Teffont to be with Rose and Fred. Rose's father, or 'Pop' as he became affectionately known, tried to help around the house and took over the vegetable garden from Fred. He also helped with jobs such as cleaning out the pheasant feeding trays and washing eggs. In the winter he would pluck any chickens and pheasants ready for the cooking pot. Occasionally, things did not go according to plan. Fred had been negotiating with some feed suppliers for a large quantity of pheasant feed. One of them had been quite persistent and rang one day when Fred and Rose were not at home. Pop answered the call. The salesman was quite underhand and told Pop that he had Fred's feed ready. Pop told him to '*Bring it on then.*' Fred was furious when he found out what had happened. Fred rang the salesman and told him in no uncertain terms to cancel the order and that he would never order feed from them again. Pop was told never in future to answer the phone!

Pop helped out around the house, including helping with the vegetable garden. In his heyday, Pop had worked as a gardener for a number of people. Many a time he entered flower show competitions and won prizes for his vegetables, often winning the overall cup. It was not unknown for him to 'borrow' vegetables from others, including Fred, if he thought they were better specimens than his own. Fred's runner beans came best in show on one occasion! This often led to conversations and lively discussions on who could grow the biggest, longest and straightest of something. This gentle banter went on for years. When Pop was in his 80s he was perplexed by a TV advert for potato crisps that showed a gardener digging up a packet of crisps. Fred could not resist the opportunity to set Pop up. A packet of crisps was carefully buried under the next root of potatoes to be dug. Pop was sent out to dig the day's supply of potatoes while the rest of the family, including Fred, hid behind the fence. When Pop's fork dug up the crisps he scratched his head and exclaimed in his broadest Wiltshire accent, '*Well, how the bloody hell did they get there? Here Rose, look what I found!*' Rose dutifully played her part, exclaiming, '*Well I never!*' Poor Pop never lived this down.

It was around this time that the first of many 'boys' came to work with Fred. There were a number of farms and estates in the country that wanted single-handed gamekeepers and there were fewer estates employing multiple keepers. It was difficult for youngsters to get the experience they needed to apply for these jobs. Sparsholt Agricultural College had started a one-year course for aspiring gamekeepers, but before they could start they had to have a year's experience working with a gamekeeper. Commander Bruce and Fred agreed to take a boy on. They would work for five days a week and get lodging on the estate. Fred didn't have any spare bedrooms so the boys stayed with one of the farm workers, but they had all their meals with Fred. So Rose was now catering for five adults every day.

The first boy to arrive was Bernard. He was quite a thin, weak-looking young man, but was keen to learn. He was always hungry and ate huge amounts of food, often to the amusement and astonishment of the family. After a shoot, Rose always provided a tea for any of the beaters that wanted to come in. There were always sausage rolls, sandwiches and – beaters' favourite – hot mince pies. Derek watched, amazed, as Bernard chomped his way through 17 mince pies after one shoot.

This was also Fred's first experience of having a young man working for him. Fred was a stickler for time, so the boys soon learnt never to be late. One of the lessons the boys had to quickly learn was how to handle guns properly. This lesson was not taken in thoroughly by Bernard and nearly led to tragic consequences. Fred was away for the day on a fox shoot on a neighbouring estate. Bernard turned up at the house, very shaken, having had a nasty experience with a gun going off. The result had left a scorch mark up his right side from his hip to his shoulder. Rose rang the boss's house and Alistair Bruce, the youngest son, came. He called an ambulance and Bernard was taken into hospital for a check-up. Luckily, there was no serious damage. The police were informed as a gun was involved. However, Bernard would not tell what had happened; when questioned, he just kept repeating *'I'm not telling.'* Clearly he had been doing something wrong and he was not going to own up to it. From the position of the scorch marks he could not have been holding the gun correctly when it went off. Maybe he had been climbing through a fence or playing soldiers, Fred never found out. Fred simply told him, *'If you are going to shoot yourself, make a bloody better job of it next time!'* Bernard was a very lucky young man; a half inch the other way and he would have been killed. He certainly had a lot of respect for guns after that. He never became a gamekeeper but instead joined the Metropolitan Police Force, first as a mounted policeman and then as a member of the special patrol group in Brixton.

Another boy that worked with Fred was a young man from Beaulieu in the New Forest. He was a fresh-faced young man who enjoyed the country life and enjoyed working with Fred. In the middle of the rearing season, Fred had a phone call from Mrs Bruce. She had been looking after a friend's Red Macaw Parrot; it was worth a great deal of money and had escaped! She wanted Fred to help capture it. The first day it had flown onto a neighbouring estate and could be heard squawking in the trees. Fred spent some time trying to find it but to no avail.

He was not best amused as this was his busiest time of year and he had to go looking for, in his words, a *'bloody parrot'*. The following morning Mrs Bruce rang to say the parrot had been seen in Hampage. She had to go to London for the day but she did have a cage with a smaller parrot in it that could be used to help entice the macaw into it. So, after lunch, Fred took Nigel to Hampage. They found the parrot sitting in a tree. The cage was put below the tree and Nigel was told to stand guard a few feet away and, if the parrot came down, to capture it. About four hours later Fred went back to Hampage, taking Nigel his tea, and found the boy sound asleep and the parrot still up the tree. Nigel was given short shrift and resumed his guard duties for few hours more. The parrot was not impressed by their efforts so had another night of freedom. Later on the third day of the parrot's escape, Mrs Bruce rang again to say the police had rung to tell her that the parrot had turned up in a garden a mile up the road near the New Inn pub. The owners had been sitting looking out of their window when the parrot landed on their bird table. Fred got his net and went off in pursuit of the bird. Luckily it was still there and he was able to capture it. Fred was wearing thick gloves, which was just as well because as he was taking it out of the net to put it in a sack the parrot grabbed his finger and bit very hard. Fred shouted, *'You bastard!'* The parrot was returned safely and a grateful Mrs Bruce gave Fred £50 for his efforts, Nigel got £10 for, as Fred put it, falling asleep all afternoon, and the people who owned the house where the parrot was captured were given a very large bottle of whisky. After that, when Fred saw Mrs Bruce's gardener he joked, *'Let that bugger out again.'*

Chapter 6

Fred kept in touch with many of the boys and helped many to get jobs. The boy that Fred kept closest contact with was Nigel Symes. Nigel came from Winchester, so did not live on the estate, but came every weekday and just had lunch and tea with the family. Nigel showed the most aptitude for gamekeeping and quickly took on board what Fred showed him. This was just as well, as Nigel's support was invaluable when Fred suffered a brain hemorrhage in 1978 at the age of 54 years.

It was a Saturday and there was a shoot. Fred had got up early and was out doing his rounds on the estate on his tractor when he started to feel ill. He managed to drive home and staggered indoors. At the time he thought he was going down with a nasty bout of flu, and went to bed. Derek came, as he was going to be a beater, but instead he took over organising the beaters and Fred's side of the shoot, helped by Nigel. As the morning wore on it was obvious that Fred was very poorly, so Rose rang for the doctor. When the doctor examined Fred they knew immediately what was wrong and phoned for an ambulance. Fred was taken into Winchester hospital; this was the week before Christmas.

He remained in hospital for the next six weeks, at one point being transferred to Southampton Hospital for a few days before returning to Winchester. He suffered a second stroke in hospital but recovered. His time in hospital was very stressful for the family, although there were some funny moments. Fred was delirious a lot of the time and was not able to think clearly or logically. One night he heard gunshots and immediately wanted to go off in search of the poachers. The nurses had to keep him in his bed. The next day when some of his keeper friends visited him they confirmed that there had indeed been poachers in the meadow behind the hospital the night before. Commander Bruce visited Fred one afternoon when Rose was sitting by his bedside. Fred was very aggressive and swore profusely at his boss, something for which he later apologised. At this time Fred was totally unaware of what he was doing or saying and had no recollection of anything he had said or done. On Christmas Day he rang Rose and said he wanted a bottle of sherry for the nurses. The best Rose could do was take a bottle that had been opened but was nearly full. This was taken into the hospital in the morning. Later in the afternoon, when Derek and Pop went to visit him, he was sitting up in bed, drinking it!

While Fred was in hospital, back at home things were far from easy. A couple of days after Fred had been taken ill there was some heavy snow, which blocked the roads. Marion had managed to battle home through the snow in her mini but had arrived home with a broken fan belt. Commander Bruce was very kind throughout this time, and paid for Marion's car to be repaired and told Rose she was to let him know if there was anything she needed. A few weeks before he was taken ill, Fred had bought Jilly, the Springer Spaniel. She was a delight, but needed to be taken out several times a day, a job shared by Marion and Nigel. She loved the snow, especially the big snowdrifts. Jilly was to become one of Fred's best dogs and when he came out of hospital he spent a lot of time training her. The remaining shoots of the season carried on with Derek taking charge and Nigel doing all the work in between. Luckily it was only the smaller cock shoots that had to be done.

When Fred came out of hospital he was still far from well and was told he would not be able to work for several months. Fred was lucky that his stroke had not caused any physical disabilities, although he did over the following year have a couple of scares when he lost his sight for short periods. His short-term memory was also poor and he had difficulty concentrating. The main problem for the family was his sudden change of mood and personality. When in one of these 'black moods' he was aggressive and bad tempered and often accused people of lying to him. This was primarily due to a lack of short-term memory and Fred having to come to terms with his condition. He also suffered severe headaches. Sometimes he would take himself to bed for a few hours. These black moods were to go on for the next two years, gradually getting less frequent and less severe in nature. Thankfully, Fred never lost his sense of humour; however, he never regained the ability to concentrate as well as he had before the stroke.

Although Fred had been told he could not go back to work for several months, he soon found his skills and knowledge were in demand. Towards the end of February, Nigel had started to capture pheasants for egg laying. The problem, though, was that Fred was the only one who knew how to tie the pheasants' wings. So as others captured the pheasants, Fred tied their wings. It was easy for Fred to dip in and out of the job, and that is what happened over the following year until eventually he was able to return to work fully. During that year, Nigel did most of the legwork and Fred 'supervised'. When Nigel left Matterley he went to Sparsholt College to do the gamekeeping course. One day his tutor told him that Fred had died several months ago as a result of his brain hemorrhage! To which Nigel replied, '*Well, that's odd because I saw him last night!*'

While Nigel was working with Fred there were a number of 'odd' – or as some at the time would say, 'extra-terrestrial' – sightings or events. One day, when Fred and Nigel were approaching a wood they noticed all the pheasants leaving the wood. Fred knew this was strange behaviour at that time of day, so the pair went through the wood to find what was frightening the birds. When they came out on the far side of the wood there was a large grey cigar-shaped object hovering in the sky. It made no noise but shot off at a huge speed. They returned home, very excited, but had no explanation for what they had seen. Fred certainly did not believe in 'flying saucers' or extra-terrestrial life forms, so he dismissed it as 'probably something to do with the army'.

Another phenomenon, which was to dog Fred for a number of years, was crop circles. The first crop circles to appear in Hampshire were on Matterley, in easy view of the A31. Over the years they were to appear every summer, getting more and more elaborate. Crop circles caused frenzy, and many elaborate theories were put forward to how they appeared, from landings of flying saucers to natural wind phenomena. Fred got really fed up with the number of people who wanted to come and take photographs of the circles or examine them. He often refused people access, as he didn't want folk trampling over the fields, destroying crops and disturbing his birds. He was always convinced that people trampling the crop down made the circles, and in his view they should be prosecuted for the damage caused.

Fred continued working full-time, seven days a week, until he was 63-years-old. He was a bit more circumspect about the amount of strenuous manual labour he could do and often supervised his 'boys' while they carried out whatever task Fred had given them. Doctors advised Fred to retire, so he settled for the next two years working part-time, five days a week with reduced hours. This would take him to the age of 65 when he could retire with a full pension. The estate recruited a new gamekeeper and Fred assisted him, or became the 'boy' as he put it.

Fred, Rose and Pop had to move out of their cottage that had been their home for 20 years to allow the new gamekeeper to move in. The family was given a three-bedroom bungalow on another part of the estate, next door to Commander Bruce. The bungalow had a lovely garden that looked out over a field of llamas, part of Mrs Bruce's menagerie. The llamas were a constant nuisance to Fred and Jilly the dog, as they would spit at them as Fred worked in the garden. Of course, this was a great source of amusement for the rest of the family. Fred and Rose could have remained living in the bungalow for the rest of their days but they wanted to return 'home' to Salisbury.

In February 1989, shortly after his 65th birthday, Fred, Rose and Pop left Matterley to live on a housing estate in

Salisbury. They were swapping the country life to live in town in a two-bedroom ground floor flat. Those that knew them were very dubious as to whether they would like the town life. But they should not have been concerned, as they took to it quite readily. Rose loved it. Dot, her close friend from her primary school days, lived around the corner and there was a small shop and doctor's surgery within a few minutes' walking distance. This gave Rose a level of independence she had not had for years. Pop by now was in his 90s and needed more care, so much of Rose's time was spent looking after him.

In early retirement, Fred was very active. He still had many friends and contacts from the local farming and shooting community. In Burcombe, the farmer Mick Coombes – son of Fred's first boss, Jack Coombes – allowed Fred to take himself off every morning with his dog, Jilly, and go for long walks over the downs and around the punch bowl where Fred had caught rabbits as a boy. Fred also wanted more garden than he had at his flat in Salisbury and Nick Coombes, Mick's son, was happy for him to take over his vegetable plot at his house. This was very handy as Fred's brother, Joby, lived next door to Nick, so a cup of tea was always on hand. In later years when Nick moved to Burcombe Manor, Fred moved his garden too and established a vegetable plot there. Fred also went fishing; something he enjoyed but had never had the time to do when he was working. He was allowed to go fishing at Burcombe and Langford but was not allowed to catch trout. However, occasionally one would find its way into his fishing bag; how it got there he never knew!

In the winter months Fred would go picking-up at a number of shoots – Wilton Park, Teffont, Broadchalk and Hurdcott. Fred knew the gamekeepers on these estates and they were very keen to have somebody of Fred's experience on the shoot. They were also keen to have his dogs, because Fred always had good working dogs. Shortly after going to Salisbury, Fred had bought himself another Labrador, Brock. He lived, along with Jilly the spaniel, in the flat with Fred, Rose and Pop. Brock was put with another Labrador for breeding and one of the puppies – Crumble – was bought by Nick Coombes. However, Nick did not have time to exercise his dog so Fred would collect Crumble every day when he went on his walk, and he also trained her. She became one of the best gundogs Fred ever had. Fred soon acquired another dog for his walks. He had a reputation for training dogs. Nick's father-in-law had bought a Labrador puppy but soon found she was too much to handle, so every day the puppy, Teal, was brought to Burcombe to be trained by Fred and to accompany him on his walks. When Fred's own dogs, Jilly and Brock, died, Crumble and Teal took their places and worked picking-up on the shoots. Fred thought the world of his dogs and they in turn thought the world of him. When Jilly and Brock died, he buried them in a copse overlooking the Punch Bowl and the oak tree that Fred had planted at the turn of the millennium in 2000.

Fred continued to go picking-up in winter months well into his 80s. He eventually had to give up when ill health intervened. Fred had suffered for some time with back and leg pain and eventually it became so bad that he could no longer cope with a full day and the walking involved. He had two major back operations to try to solve the problems but neither operation was successful. So Fred had soldiered on, enduring the pain with some relief from painkillers and steroid injections. Fred's experience and knowledge has always been in demand, though, and over the years fellow gamekeepers have often sought his advice on a range of shooting topics.

Chapter 7

Fred's forthright views on some of the issues facing the countryside were based on a lifetime of living and working in the woods and the fields. He was particularly challenged by the impact of what he calls 'do-gooders and experts'.

When Fred was a boy, and in his keepering days, he loved to hear and see the songbirds, butterflies and bees. There were flocks of green finches, sparrows and lapwings. All manner of small birds would come and feed from the grain he scattered for the pheasants. The numbers of these birds have been decimated over the last 30 years. This is often put down to environmental changes such as farmers using sprays, which kill off the insects. These might have some effect but Fred was convinced that the largest problem by far is the rise in the number of vermin caused by the over-protection of some animals and birds of prey. He argued that if intensive farming were the problem why has there been a decline in songbirds and ground birds in forests and on the moors where there is no intensive farming?

The worst vermin in my opinion are foxes and badgers. Badgers were particularly bad where I was. We killed a terrific amount of badgers in my time and everywhere we went and every time we did the wild bird population increased. I'm not

*just talking about game birds; it's the other birds
like blackbirds, that sort of thing. I've been up a
hedgerow in the morning after a badger has been
up there. They've had every nest, every wasp
nest, every bumblebee nest, every bird nest and
every egg up the hedgerow. They've had the lot,
not missed one! There's not a bumblebee nest left
in the countryside now, they dig them up for the
honey. They'll have the hedgehogs too; they just
eat the guts, not the prickly bits. They'll get all the
ground-nesting birds; eat the eggs and the chicks
too. They're moaning about not having enough
bees to pollinate the plants but it's the badgers
doing that! These do-gooders have no sense!*

Fred had a hierarchy of vermin that, in his view, caused the
most damage in the countryside:

Badgers
Foxes
Goss hawks
Stoats and weasels
Sparrow hawks
Carrion crows
Rooks, jackdaws and magpies

All of these creatures steal eggs and the chicks in the nest.
Birds of prey such as goss hawks and sparrow hawks also
kill smaller birds. One morning after Fred had retired he was

out walking in Burcombe where he grew up. He stopped and started talking to another man who was also out for a walk. As they chatted, a sparrow hawk flew between them. Fred exclaimed, *'Good God, look at that.'* *'Yes, isn't it marvellous,'* came the reply. Fred said, *'Yes, but there are too many of them, there are two pairs in this village.'* The man replied, *'But they only have one bird each day.'* Fred's reply was, *'That's 365 for each bird, times that by four! That goes for all the hawks and birds of prey.'*

These birds, and many of the vermin, are now protected, but they were not in Fred's day. Much of his time was spent in controlling the vermin on the estates where he worked. A lot of poisons were used, although Fred never used one of the deadliest; strychnine. To get rid of foxes and badgers, Fred's preferred method was to use gas or wire traps. Smaller vermin such as stoats and weasels were caught in tunnel traps. To kill birds such as rooks and crows he would put some poison in an empty eggshell and leave it at dusk where he knew the birds would come. The next morning he would return to get rid of the poisoned egg and pick up the carcasses of any dead birds. All vermin would also be shot if he had his gun with him. Sometimes the unfortunate creature was killed by unconventional means. One day, Fred was walking down a ride in the wood carrying a bucket and spreading feed for his pheasants. A sparrow hawk flew down and Fred swung his bucket and knocked it to the ground and then killed it by stamping on it. The conventional way for catching sparrow hawks was with a sawyer trap, which was made for the purpose. The trap would catch the bird alive and Fred would then dispatch it.

These methods of catching vermin were legal in Fred's working life. Many of them are still legal; you can still set wires to catch vermin, for example, but you cannot use gin traps as these are illegal. Most lay people do not know the law regarding the catching and killing of vermin and will call foul if they see a trap or wire. As Fred rightly says, there are fewer and fewer people who know the country ways. So-called do-gooders are obsessed with protecting birds of prey and in Fred's words, 'animals that kill other animals'. This rise in vermin has corresponded with the fall in smaller unprotected species of birds, animals and insects. Fred was of the strong opinion that if you want to save the countryside and see more songbirds, hedgehogs and bumblebees, then vermin must be controlled. He never killed an animal or bird for pleasure. For him, it was a necessary function – to either keep a balance or provide food. In his day there were always plenty of foxes, badgers and birds of prey but their numbers were controlled and other creatures had a chance to thrive. As Fred often said, '*Nobody wants a countryside where there are no foxes, badgers or birds of prey, but there are just too many of them now.*'

Fred also wanted to see the reverse of the ban on foxhunting. He was never a keen foxhunter. In fact, he wouldn't let the foxhounds come on to the estates where he lived, not because of the foxes but the hounds followed by a menagerie of assorted horses charging across the fields damaging the ground and damaging the shoot. There have recently been some disturbing films of what appears to be individuals carrying out cruel practices by giving fox cubs to hounds. Fred has no time for these people or this kind of practice. He too thinks it is cruel. *'Trouble is, there are always stupid people out there. They show it on television and then people think it's common practice and everybody is doing it, which they aren't.'*

He also had no time for what he referred to as 'do gooders and so-called experts'. *'They haven't a clue,'* he would say, *'no common sense.'* He would recount a story that illustrated his point. Somebody from Bristol had driven down to Hampshire and released about half a dozen hand-reared foxes. Fred went out and found these foxes wandering about in broad daylight and shot them all. Whoever had released them had not thought through the consequences of releasing tame foxes onto a very successful pheasant shoot!

The ways of the gamekeeper have changed a great deal over the years. Shoots are often now seen as a way of making a large income for the estate rather than the pastime and pleasure of the boss and his guests. Pheasant eggs are hatched on large game farms and day-old chicks are bought to rear. Farms have become highly mechanised and the farm workers' cottages have filled with well-off town folk. A large number seem to have a picture book ideal of the country life and have little understanding of how the countryside they enjoy has come about in the first place. In Fred's view, this lack of knowledge and understanding has led to detrimental changes in country life and thus a fall in the wild populations of birds and small mammals.

Fred's passion for the countryside never diminished. He loved to hear the skylarks and watch the flocks of green finches. He would often lament that *'These people, all they want to do is protect the bloody birds of prey! What about the poor little songbirds, why don't they protect them?'*

Fred's ashes are to be scattered on the downs he loved at Burcombe amongst the wild thyme and cowslips. It is a tranquil place which still beats to the rhythm of the seasons. A fitting last resting place for a true old countryman.